Table of Contents

Chapter 1 - Introduction   3

Chapter 2 - Meditation In Religion   7

Chapter 3 - Meditation to Relieve Stress   11

Chapter 4 - Meditation to Relieve Depression   16

Chapter 5 - Meditation As A Healing Tool   19

Chapter 6 - Meditation To Induce Sleep   22

Chapter 7 - Meditation For Inner Peace   26

Chapter 8 - Meditation To Relieve Back Pain   28

Chapter 9 - Meditation To Become A Better Person   31

Chapter 10 - Meditating For Love   34

Chapter 11 - Meditate Yourself Free From Addiction   38

Chapter 12 - Meditation To Cast Out Negativity   41

Chapter 13 - Meditation And Aromatherapy   43

Chapter 14 - Using Meditation To Improve Concentration   45

Chapter 15 - Practicing Meditation For A Healthy Life   47

Chapter 16 - Meditation Retreats and Lessons   49

Chapter 1 - Introduction

What is meditation? When you hear this word you often think about someone sitting cross legged and chanting. You probably associate meditation with Eastern religions such as Buddhism and the reason for this practice to achieve "higher consciousness."

Meditation is rooted in basically all religions. It is used in a variety of different ways, has many techniques and is practiced for a variety of different purposes. Today, even medical doctors will advocate this relaxation technique for those who are suffering from anxiety or depression.

Physical exercise is almost like a physical cure all. Exercise can help your heart, stave off certain cancers, prevent diseases that attack the obese like diabetes and stroke, can raise your energy level as well as your spirits. Most doctors today advocate physical exercise to any patient who is able to participate. No one will say that exercise is harmful.

Think about meditation as an exercise for your brain. It can be used the same way, especially when it comes to alleviating stress, anxiety and mild depression. Meditation is to the mind what physical exercise is to the body. At catch all to prevent or cure some mental conditions.

It is estimated that one in four Americans suffer from a mental disorder of some kind. One in 17 Americans suffer from a mental disorder that is so severe that it renders them disabled. The number one culprit is depression, which is almost the father of all neurosis. Depression is the second most common reason why people are on disability in America (the first being back pain which is sometimes related to stress).

The one in four Americans who suffer from mental disorders is an estimate based upon those who go to the doctor for treatment. Many more people suffer from these disorders without seeking medical attention because they fear the stigma of being labeled as "crazy." They self medicate themselves in bars and taverns with alcohol, drugs or other destructive methods.

Meditation can help with depression. It can help with anxiety and other minor mental disorders from which so many people seem to be suffering. In addition, meditation can give you spiritual relief, help lower blood pressure and even give you more energy. Meditation will not do you any harm but has everything to offer.

This is not a guide on using meditation as a substitute for medical treatment. Rather, it should be used along with medical treatment so that you can achieve better results. In the case of minor anxiety (as in the case you are worrying about a test at school) you can use meditation to calm yourself instead of using tranquilizers or alcohol - both of which are addictive and self destructive.

Meditation can be practiced anywhere. You do not have to trek up to the Himalayan Mountains in order to meditate. You do not need to sit cross legged on the floor. You do not even need to sit on the floor.

You just have to find a quiet place where you can cleanse your mind. If you do this for about 10 minutes every day, you will start to notice a difference in your mind. This works the same way as an exercise regime.

Many people reject the idea of meditation because they think it is quackery and "too much trouble." After all, when you're upset, you can easily find relief from popping a tranquilizer or taking a stiff drink. It can be difficult for someone to change their habits. But once you begin a regime of meditation, you will no longer look at this time as something that you "have to do" but as a time when you can truly relax.

Meditation has been practiced for over 5,000 years. It is a tried and true form of relaxation and a way to achieve inner peace. Always a popular remedy in Eastern religions, meditation is becoming more of a common practice in the West.

Once you learn a little something about this Eastern healing art and form of spiritual self awareness, you can begin to practice on your own. As is the case with physical exercise, once you get into the routine, you will begin to feel results right away and look forward to your time when you can practice this ancient way of seeking inner peace.

When you begin to meditate, give it a fair shot. This is not something that works overnight. In today's society, we are always looking for immediate gratification. The instant pill that cures all. The instant diet. The instant bit of help. Meditation is not immediate gratification. You will feel better after you have practiced it, even after the first time. But it takes a while before you begin to start feeling the full benefits.

Start out slowly with meditation and then work your way up. You should start out with five minutes at a time. Gradually, you can work yourself up to about 30 minutes. You do not have to meditate for hours or days on end to achieve results. You can do it on your lunch hour and get results right away, once you have learned the basic techniques.

This book will detail some ways you can use meditation to help yourself through difficulties as well as become a better person. We are all striving for improvement. Meditation is one way that we can help ourselves achieve not only spiritual well being, but emotional, physical and psychological well being as well. It costs nothing to begin this practice and can be done anywhere. This book will teach you techniques on how to get started in your amazing journey through the world of meditation.

Chapter 2 - Meditation In Religion

Before we begin with actual meditation techniques for healing and enlightenment, it is essential that you learn a bit about the history of meditation. Although most people associate this with the Eastern philosophies and arts, meditation has a root in virtually all of the major religions in the world. While not all of them practice chanting and crossing their legs, the concept of meditation is evidenced in most religious practices, even today.

Hinduism is one of the world's oldest religions and where meditation first developed more than 5,000 years ago. Millions of people practice meditation techniques as taught in Hinduism. In the Hindi religion, Yoga is considered to be the main philosophy. Those practicing meditation in accordance with Hinduism learn the six schools of Yoga that teach both inner and outer well being.

In Hinduism, meditation is used to reach a calm state of mind. It is used to diminish erratic thoughts and focus on one thought so that you can pay attention. According to Hindu philosophy, there are five different states of mind, four of which block focus. Ksipta is the first state of mind which describes a mind that is filled with agitation. The second state of mind is Mudha where a person has a problem getting information to reach their brain - they may be considered absentminded because their thoughts are in a jumble.

In Viksipta the mind is able to receive information, but has trouble processing it into thought. A person who experiences Ekagra, which is the fourth state of mind, is calm and able to focus. This moves to the last state of mind which is Nirodha where the person is able to focus and able to concentrate on what they are doing.

Meditation is used in prayer rituals in Hinduism as well as Hatha Yoga, which is a state of physical postures that are used to raise spiritual awareness. The positions that you will often see described in yoga are called chakras. The most common is the lotus position in which a person sits cross legged with their ankles on their legs.

A mantra is also used in meditation as part of the Hindu faith. The mantra can be repeated out loud as a chant or can be repeated in your head. In Hinduism, meditation is the key to finding not only spiritual awareness, but also higher knowledge.

In the Bahai religion, meditation is also used along with prayer. It is used primarily as a form of discovering the spirituality within yourself.

Buddhists also practice meditation and it figures heavily in their religion. Lord Buddha was said to have found spiritual enlightenment when meditating. There are two different types of meditation practices in Buddhism and they are both used for spiritual enlightenment. The two types of meditation are called shamatha and vispassana. They are used to focus attention and develop wisdom respectively.

In Buddhism, the objective of the traditions is enlightenment and self awareness. This is achieved in a number of ways, most often through meditation.

While Eastern religions use meditation as a way to gain enlightenment and tend to focus on one object during their practice, Western religions tend to focus on prayer when meditating. Christianity has three main facets - Catholicism, Orthodox and Protestant. In the Catholic faith, saying the rosary is a form of meditation as a person is deeply engrossed in prayer and is supposed to be putting their full concentration in the prayer. Orthodox Christians also rely heavily upon prayer. In many protestant faiths, remembering verses from the bible are used as a way to achieve focus on prayer.

Christianity will not outwardly embrace meditation in the form of words. Unlike Eastern religions, Western religions are not as open to other faiths. Meditation and the practice of any other philosophy is usually considered wrong in most Christian faiths. However, the practice is still somewhat the same.

Islam was one of the first religions to use meditation as a form of healing. The prophet Muhammad spent hours meditating and there are two different schools of meditation taught in Islam. Tadabbur is the first school of meditation that is accepted by all Muslim scholars and is used to achieve a higher level from God. This is used to submit to the will of Allah. The second school is called Sufi meditation and is not accepted by all Muslim scholars. From noon to sunset, Muslims will meditate during the second stage of Hajj.

In Judaism, meditation goes back thousands of years to Isaac who is said to meditate. In both Kabbalah and Hassidic philosophies, meditation is practiced as "boded" through the book of understanding. Kabbalah has gained popularity over the recent years and relies heavily upon meditation.

Other religions that also practice meditation include Jainism, Sikhism and Taoism, both Eastern religions. While meditation is a form of achieving inner peaces in the Eastern religions, it is mostly used as a form of prayer in the Western religions such as Judaism, Christianity and Islam.

In the west today, meditation is practiced in some newer religions such as spiritualism and new age philosophies. In secular societies, meditation is also used for a variety of purposes, including as a healing art. In secular meditation, there is no mysticism involved nor any directive to achieve spiritual enlightenment. It is used mostly for healing and well being.

In addition to using meditation for different purposes, each religion that practices meditation also has a distinct way of practicing meditation. In many cultures, beads are used in meditation. This is true of Catholics who use rosary beads as well as Muslims who use prayer beads. Both Hindu and Buddhists religions also implement the use of rosary beads. Beads are often used to allow the person to concentrate on a fixed object. Although the fixed object is the beads in the Eastern religions, the fixed object in Christianity and Islam is God or Allah.

For over 5,000, meditation has been used for a variety of purposes. Despite the differences, the similarities remain the same and that is that meditation can be used to achieve a calmer and clearer state of mind.

Chapter 3 - Meditation to Relieve Stress

One of the primary purposes for which meditation is used today in the West is to relieve stress. As Americans become more stressed out all of the time, they seek ways to achieve relief. Many people are looking for something to help them instead of taking pills or alcohol.

Stress is the biggest medical crisis that we face today. With so many people looking for a cure to relieve themselves of stress, doctors are handing out tranquilizers like they were candy. Yet people continue to be stressed.

Continued stress plays havoc on your central nervous system as well as your immune system. It can lower your immune system so that all diseases are virtually invited into your body. Why mess with stress when you can use meditation to help you?

Even the medical community will admit that meditation is good for stress. While most medical professionals will scoff at the idea of any type of alternative healing method, meditation is one that most of them can see benefits. It certainly cannot cause any harm and has actually been proven to help you relax.

Meditation can relieve stress. It does work, but it takes practice. In order to use meditation to relieve stress and anxiety, do the following:

1. Find a quiet place where you can sit and relax that is peaceful. This can be anywhere in your house. Once you get used to meditating, you will be able to do this anywhere, even at your office desk. To start,

look for a tranquil place in the home.

2. Sit in a comfortable position. If you can sit cross legged on the ground, fine. If not, sit in another comfortable position. You want to be relaxed, but not to the point that you fall asleep. Make sure that you are sitting up so that you do not fall asleep. You want to clear your head, not fall asleep.

3. Clear your head of thoughts. One of the things that stresses people out is intrusive thoughts. This is what causes mental stress. You are worried about money, your job, the laundry, what to cook for dinner, if you have a dress for a party, is the vacuum cleaner broken, etc. In order for meditation to be effective, you have to clear your head of these intrusive thoughts.

It is not always easy to clear your head. This is why so many people use a mantra when meditating. A trick to clearing your head is to concentrate solely on a particular object. You can also find a word that you like to use and make it your own "mantra." Clearing your head takes practice, but once you are able to achieve this, the world of meditation is truly open to you.

4. Each time an intrusive thought comes into your mind, let it go. Imagine yourself tossing it into the garbage can. Concentrate on the object instead. Continue to do this until the object has your total concentration.

5. While you are practicing this form of total concentration, also practice breathing techniques. Take a deep breath in through your

mouth, hold it for five seconds and then breathe out through your nose. You can also concentrate on the breathing technique as your "object."

6. Do not expect miracles the first time you try this. Meditation takes practice. Does it work to relax you? Yes. It's been working for 5,000 years to relax people so chances are that it will work on you as well. Start with a small session and then gradually work your way up.

7. Incense can also be combined with meditation. Using incense is pleasant and will make the experience more pleasant as well. You can also use soothing music during your meditation practice as well.

8. Schedule a time to meditate each and every day. This will be difficult at first as you will have to endure a change in your daily routine. It will be worth it in the long run as the meditation starts to work. Once you find the meditation actually working, it is like a light going on in a dark room. You will not only want to make time for mediation, but you will look forward to this daily ritual.

Even medical doctors will acknowledge that meditation, especially when combined with breathing techniques, is good for you and can relieve stress. There are indications that it lowers the blood pressure as well as boosts the immune system. The breathing exercises stimulate oxygen to your brain and clearing your head allows the intrusive thoughts that plague and worry you to be eliminated.

There are a variety of different reasons why people suffer from stress. The world today is not the world of 50 years ago where things moved at a much slower pace. Everything moves fast and most of us bite off more than we can chew in the never ending search for getting "the world and everything in it."

Stress can be a precursor to a variety of different illnesses, even cancer. It lowers the immune system and allows disease to traipse into your body. Yet the cures for stress can be even more detrimental to your health than the stress itself. Tranquilizers, which are often prescribed for stress, are highly addictive and have serious side effects. On top of that, there is always a danger of an accidental overdose. Many people take tranquilizers with alcohol to achieve results that constantly seem to require more medication. We constantly hear of people who die due to this lethal combination.

To date, no one has meditated themselves to death. Although, this ancient art is addictive, but in a positive way. You may find that you prefer to meditate over watching television and want to continue with this practice. You may also find that you wish to learn more about this ancient art and begin studying the practice of meditation through the ages and try to achieve enlightenment or a purpose in life. Although this can be addictive and time consuming, it is far from harmful and can really change your life for the better.

If you are suffering from stress or anxiety, you may be tempted to take tranquilizers or even a drink. After all, they are the fastest and most convenient cure for the condition. Try meditation first and be sure to give it a full shot before you resort to harmful pills or alcohol. Meditation can relieve stress and anxiety.

Chapter 4 - Meditation to Relieve Depression

The medical community is up in the air when it comes to meditation to relieve depression. Most doctors will quickly prescribe anti-depressants to anyone who suffers from depression, whether it is mild or severe.

There are some doctors who believe that those with mental illness should not meditate because it can lead to schizophrenia. There is no medical evidence that anything leads to this disease that has proven to be a biological condition that is often inherited. This idea stems from a story of someone who meditated for a long period of time and then went on to develop schizophrenia. This is totally misleading information and much more likely to be an urban legend. Schizophrenia is a biological disorder and all the mediation in the world is not going to make you develop this disease.

Depression is usually the root of anxiety. There are many theories as to why depression seems to be at an all time high, particularly in the United States. There are literally millions of people in the United States who are on medication for depression.

Severe depression is a serious condition and should be treated by a medical doctor. There are a variety of ways to treat severe depression, including therapy and medication. However, using meditation in addition to these methods can give one a sense of control. In cases of mild depression, using meditation can also alleviate some of the symptoms of this disease.

Many mental illnesses and conditions stem from a loss of control felt on behalf of the patient. People who suffer from depression often resort to self medicating with illegal drugs or alcohol to numb themselves to the symptoms. Meditation can give someone a sense of control in their life, which many people with depression so desperately need.

In the medical community, anything other than medicine for depression is usually frowned upon. Medical doctors will prescribe pills such as Zoloft in an effort to "cure" depression. They will also advise that you seek counseling. If the pills do not work, they will continue to prescribe pills until they get the right combination. Many people end up not ever getting out of the depressive state.

Medical doctors will stress the dangers of treating depression with anything other than medication. They stress that depression is a chemical imbalance in the brain. If this is the case, there can be no harm at all in trying meditation to treat this common disorder. Depression often goes hand in hand with anxiety, so at the very least, you can expect it to relax you.

To practice meditation to treat depression, find a quiet room and sit down, closing your eyes. Follow the simple instructions in the prior chapter for meditating. By concentrating on this every day for about 20 minutes, you can alleviate some of the symptoms of depression.

In addition to practicing meditation to alleviate depression, you should also exercise. Some doctors will advise exercise to those who suffer from depression. Exercise will raise your endorphins and increase serotonin levels, which is what medication basically does.

Unlike medications that are used to combat depression, meditation does not have any side effects and will not, after a long period of use, harm your liver. If you suffer from serious depression and have been prescribed medication for the condition, do not stop taking your medication without consulting your doctor. But you can try meditation and exercise in addition to the medication to see if you can help yourself. You may be able to gradually reduce your medication in this matter.

If you suffer from mild depression, try meditation first before racing to the doctor's office for anti depressants. As always, if you have thoughts of suicide or harming others, seek medical attention immediately.

Chapter 5 - Meditation As A Healing Tool

Meditation has been proven to be effective in boosting the immune system which is the focus of all healing. Having a healthy immune system is crucial to having good physical and mental health. Your immune system can be boosted in many different ways, including with meditation.

For thousands of years, meditation has been used in the East as a healing tool. Because it stimulates relaxation, you can use this tool to also help you heal both mentally and physically.

There are many different ways that you can use meditation to heal. There is some medical evidence that meditation can stave off disease, even cancer. However, there is not enough medical studies on this matter to prove any link between meditation and cancer survival. Suffice to say that the medical community, despite its best efforts, know very little about cancer, including why some people get this disease and others do not. They also are up in arms when it comes to a cure for most types of cancer.

Meditation will certainly not do you any harm. If you practice this ever day for about 20 minutes a day, you can relax which will, in turn, eliminate stress and enhance your immune system. One thing that has been proven regarding meditation is that it can reduce stress. And stress has been linked to disease, including cancer.

One way to use meditation on a daily basis to heal is to try the total relaxation from head to toe. In order to do this, sit in a comfortable position with your legs extended in front of you.

You can put a pillow behind your back as you practice this form of meditation. Once you have gotten comfortable, you can then begin the meditation. Close your eyes and count backwards from ten to zero.

Begin by wiggling your toes just a bit. Feel the energy in your toes and allow them to have your total concentration. Do this for about a minute or so, then move to your feet. Again, give your feet your total concentration and feel the energy contained in this part of your body.

Continue to do this until you work your way up to the top of your head. Be sure to practice breathing techniques as you work on this exercise. Breathing in through your mouth and out through your nose. The entire exercise should take about 20 minutes.

Try to continue to concentrate on the parts of your body while you practice this form of healing meditation. With each part of your body that you focus on, say aloud "this is well" or "this is perfect." You can use a variation to this, but what you want to do is give affirmation that each part of your body is in perfect condition. Saying this aloud a few times gives an affirmation.

This is a good way to meditate without worrying about your mind wandering. Instead of trying to allow your mind to go blank, you can concentrate on good health. Like attracts like, so says the laws of the universe. If you tell yourself that everything is well, everything can be well.

Using affirmations with meditation can help you heal not only physically, but mentally as well. Make sure that you tell yourself that you are happy. Happiness, after all, is really a frame of mind. If you can manage to control the instinct to be happy through meditation, you can achieve not only happiness, but health as well.

While meditation should not take the place of traditional medicine when it comes to healing, it can be used in conjunction with traditional medicine so that you can relieve stress from your body and improve your body's immune system. Studies on cancer patients who used meditation as opposed to those who did not use meditation indicate that those who meditated lived longer than those who did not use this practice.

Meditation has been effective as a healing tool for thousands of years. This is but one technique that you can use in meditating that will allow you to promote self healing.

Chapter 6 - Meditation To Induce Sleep

If you are like most people, you have suffered at times from sleeplessness. Insomnia plagues most of us at one time or another and has a variety of different causes. Most people opt to take medication when insomnia becomes too much of a burden to bear.

Medication to treat insomnia can be dangerous in that it is addictive. Although there are newer medications on the market today that are supposed to be less addictive than traditional medications, they still warn that they can form a dependency. When you form a dependency on any medication, your body needs more and more of the pills to achieve the same effect. Sleeping pills are supposed to be used for a brief time period to get your body back into a sleep pattern, but a good many Americans are using them all of the time. Sleeping pills are one of the most abused of all prescription medications.

If you want to get to sleep naturally, you can try meditation. Meditation to eliminate insomnia is very effective and is not dangerous like taking sleeping pills. On top of that, no one has ever died from an overdose of meditation.

To effective meditate to overcome insomnia, do the following:

1. Lie in a comfortable position on your bed. Make sure that you are totally comfortable and ready to go to sleep.

2. Close your eyes and start concentrating on the most pleasant place that you can think about. Your own personal utopia where everything

is as you want it. Start with the climate of the perfect place and begin to think of the type of home that you would have in this place and create it in your mind.

3. After you have created the place and dwelling of your personal utopia, start incorporating what type of scent would greet you at the door when you walk into your utopia. Would it be a soft perfume or the smell of something good cooking in the oven?

4. Start incorporating what type of furnishings you would have in this personal utopia. Right down to the color of the sofa.

5. Think about some comforts you would like to have in your own utopia. Think about LCD televisions, Ipods or other gadgets that you would like to own. While you're at it, throw in a car in the driveway. What is your dream car.

6. Bring others into the utopia. Think of who you would like to be in your world. Your family, your children, Brad Pitt, whoever. Make them part of your personal utopia.

7. Give yourself something to do in your personal utopia. What is your role in this world? Do you have a career? Do you just lounge around? Are you famous or powerful? Give this role to yourself.

Chances are, before you get to the type of clothes in your closet in your personal utopia, you will find yourself asleep. You may even dream of your own personal utopia. Each night, when you go to sleep, you can visit your own personal utopia.

Do not visit your utopia during the day. That is the trick of this meditation. Unlike other meditation that you can do whenever you want, insomnia meditation should only be used when you are ready to go to sleep. Soon, your body will associate your own personal utopia thoughts with sleep and you will be able to go to sleep when you visit this wonderful place.

Some might argue that this is merely daydreaming. Going to your own personal utopia is a sort of daydreaming, but with one difference - you are not allowing your thoughts to wander, you are controlling your thoughts. Daydreaming is usually the result of getting bored at work or school and allowing your thoughts to wander to another place.

By controlling your thoughts before you go to sleep, you may be able to control your sleep state as well. You will probably dream about your personal utopia once in a while, but not all of the time. Other things that ran through your head and made an impression on you throughout the day will be mixed in with yoru dreams.

Using meditation to fall asleep is an old practice. Have you ever heard the expression "counting sheep?" That is meditation. It relies on the same premise - you are concentrating on the sheep jumping over the fence. You remove other thoughts from your mind and allow the sheep take over. You continue to count until you fall asleep.

Counting sheep is boring. Dreaming about a magnificent home with Brad Pitt is a lot more fun. Just make sure that you visit your own personal utopia when you are going to sleep and not at work, driving or when you are supposed to be doing something else. You want to associate this pleasant place with going to sleep.

Chapter 7 - Meditation For Inner Peace

When we come into the world, we are innocent, pure and aware. As we grow into adulthood, various things happen to us to alter our basic state of being. These often conflict with inner peace. In order to get back to inner peace, we can meditate.

Meditating to achieve inner peace is often used in religious practices, especially in Eastern philosophy. This can also be used secularly as well. If you want to get back to your basic state of being, such as how innocent and joyous you were in infancy, you can do so by meditating.

In order to reconnect with your basic state, you will have to tap into your basic energy. You have to strip away the layers of negative energy that have enveloped you since you were a child. Take the following steps to use mediation and affirmation to achieve inner peace:

1. Sit in a comfortable position on the floor, preferably with your legs crossed or directly in front of you.

2. Make sure that the room is quiet and still. You do not want any distractions so this is something that is best done late in the evening or very early in the morning.

3. Start by breathing in through your mouth and out through your nose. With the first breath, think that you are breathing in courage and exhaling fear.

4. With the next breath, inhale love exhale hate. Inhale peace, exhale conflict. Inhale knowledge, exhale ignorance.

Continue this technique for about 20 minutes, repeating affirmations in your head. Affirmations, when practiced with meditation and breathing techniques can be very powerful. You will find yourself transported to how you felt when you were a child. After this 20 minutes of seeking inner peace, you will feel better.

Each time you practice this technique of meditation, you will discover that it gets easier and easier to relax. Most of us are so tense throughout the day that our bodies are almost contorted by the end of the day. This method of meditation can not only allow you to relax, but also allow you to achieve inner peace that you so desperately seek.

All religions look for some sort of peace within the soul. All seek the same purity and innocence found in childhood. Yet meditating for inner peace is not a religious experiences unless you seek it out as a religious experience. It can be used in a secular context just as easily as it can in religious philosophy. This type of meditation is what you make it.

Chapter 8 - Meditation To Relieve Back Pain

Most Americans will suffer with back pain at some point in their lives. Back pain is the most common reason why people go to the doctor. It is also the number one disability in the United States. In some cases, a slipped disc is the cause of a back injury, or a sprained muscle. In many cases, however, there is no known cause for the pain. Yet it is very real. Some doctors feel that lack of exercise is the root of back pain in America.

Before you begin an exercise routine to alleviate back pain, talk to your doctor. You want to make sure that the cause of your back pain is not something physical like a herniated disc or a sprained muscle. If this is the case, you do not want to aggravate the injury by exercising, but want to rest your back until the injury heals.

If the back pain cause is unknown, you can talk to your doctor about exercise. You will want to do crunches and other abdominal exercises as these muscles support the spine. Weak stomach, weak back is the rule of thumb.

Whether or not your back pain is caused by a physical condition or weak muscles, you can use meditation in a way to alleviate your back pain. Follow these simple rules to meditate away back pain:

1. Sit comfortably. Try to keep your posture straight.

2. Take a deep breath in through your mouth, hold it as long as you can and then breathe out through your nose. Do this six times in a row.

3. Tense your entire body up, beginning with your extremities. Start by tensing up your toes, fingers and work up to your torso. Even tense your jaw and keep your eyes wide open. Get yourself as tense as possible and hold it for about five seconds.

4. Slowly start to relieve the tension, beginning with the last part of your body that you tensed. Relieve the tension slowly throughout your entire body, right down to your fingertips. You should feel like Jello when you are finished. The entire process should take about 15 minutes.

Most of the reason that you feel pain is due to tension. By capturing the attention and then letting it go, you can eliminate the tension from your body and cause your muscles to relax. This is a great way to let go of pain and is very effective.

Doctors can do very little for your back pain. The best they can do in most cases is prescribe pain medication such as Vicodin or Tylenol with Codeine. Both of these substances are addictive, especially Vicodin.

Meditating is a lot safer than using Vicodin or other pain relief to treat back pain, especially chronic back pain. Pain medication builds up a tolerance in your system and you need more of the drug to achieve the same effect. You are not only addicted to the medication, but you are needing more and more of it to get by.

Because of lawsuits against doctors and laws regarding trafficking of Vicodin and other controlled substances, doctors are hesitant to prescribe this medication repeatedly. After a while, they will tell you that you have to "wean yourself off the drug" and send you to a pain management clinic. Pain management teaches you to deal with pain by using such techniques as…..meditation and exercises. You might as well cut to the chase and use them from the first so that you can avoid the nightmare of being addicted to opiates, such as Vicodin.

Meditation to relieve back pain works well. If the pain persists, gets worse or wakes you up at night, see your physician. Most causes of back pain are not serious, but this can be a trigger that there is something else wrong in your body.

Chapter 9 - Meditation To Become A Better Person

Most of us want to become a better person. There are very few people who do not strive for perfection among us and even fewer who think that they are perfect. Most of us realize that we have flaws and wish to become more compassionate, loving and forgiving.

You can become a better person if you practice the meditation techniques of the Dalai Lama. Some Buddhists believe him to be reincarnated from the God of Compassion. The Dalai Lama is a leader and a Nobel Peace Prize winner, but he attributes this greatness (which his humility will not allow him to acknowledge) to meditation.

The method used by the Dalai Lama is easy and can be practiced by anyone who wishes to become a better person through the use of meditation. Take the following steps towards becoming all you can be:

1. Sit comfortably and relaxed with your eyes closed. You can use the relaxation meditation if you want, or just allow your limbs and body to go limp.

2. In your mind's eyes, picture the way that you appear to others when you are at your most angry or impatient. Put this on the left side of your body and get a good visualization of yourself in this state.

3. Once you have a good visualization of your angry and impatient self, picture yourself as being happy and carefree as well as calm. Picture yourself being caring, compassionate and patient. Again, make this

a very clear image in your mind's eye and put this person on the right side of you.

4. Now that you have both images of yourself in your mind's eye - the good person who is kind and compassionate and patient and the other person who is angry and impatient, which would you rather be? Which version of yourself would you like to present to the world?

5. Practice this on a daily basis for about 10 minutes a day. Each day, add more to each of your images. Make sure that you get facial expressions correct as well as mannerisms. You can even picture yourself saying something in a certain manner.

6. What do you think about the "bad" person on the left? Do you think that this is a person others would like? Is this the person that you want to present to the world?

7. Picture the negative energy surrounding the person on the left and the positive energy surrounding the person on the right. Keep this as part of your focus as you practice this meditation each day. Remember to keep adding mannerisms and other facial expressions to each person.

8. In addition to the person on the left being angry and impatient, also allow them to be everything negative. Incorporate jealousy, envy, arrogance, rudeness, cruelness and depression in this person. Continue to incorporate positive qualities in the person on the right.

9. Once you have a clear image of the person on the right and the person on the left, you will have a clear image of who you want to be. Hopefully, it will be the person on the right. The positive energy qualities will naturally overwhelm the negative energy qualities of the person on the left. The next step is to get rid of the person on the left. Banish him or her from your life.

10. This little meditation exercise is very effective at not only making you into a better person with more positive energy, but also allowing you to become more aware of negative vs. positive behavior. There is nothing wonderful about the negative energy attributes. They do not do anything to enhance your life. The positive energy, however, is very beneficial.

Meditating your way to a becoming a better person is not done in a day. This takes time to practice. Each day, hopefully, you will discover more about yourself and the negative energy versus the positive energy and focus more on the positive.

You can practice this technique throughout your life so that you can not only become the best person that you can be, but that you can surround yourself with positive light.

Chapter 10 - Meditating For Love

As human beings, we all want love. We often say that we need food, shelter and clothing to survive, but love is also a necessity. Human beings are social animals and can become depressed if they are left alone.

Remember the film "Castaway" starring Tom Hanks? He puts a face on a ball and names it so that he can have "company" as he is shipwrecked on a deserted island. He does this in order to keep from falling apart. As a human being, he needs companionship. There are very few people who are comfortable being lonely.

If you want love, the only thing you need to do is ask for it. It is plentiful in the universe. You need to be able to open up your heart so that you can receive love, however.

This is easier said than done. Most of us have closed our hearts, especially when we are adults. We have been hurt once too often and are afraid of getting hurt again. So we shut down our hearts and reject any chance of allowing love into our lives.

Do you know someone who habitually has bad relationships? They are constantly going out with people who are unavailable, either emotionally or physically, are abusive or have a substance abuse problem? This is not an accident that they are finding these type of people. They are actively seeking out these sort of troubled relationships. This is because they feel that they do not deserve the happiness and love that is there waiting for them. Instead, they choose to look for misery.

Everyone deserves to love and be loved. And it is easy to do, too. All you have to do is open up your heart and ask for love and the universe shall provide it for you.

To meditate to get love, you need to be able to use all of your senses during your meditation practice. Do as follows:

1. Sit in a comfortable and relaxed position. For this technique, you can even lay down. You want to be as comfortable as possible when you look for love. Close you eyes.

2. Tell your body and mind that you want no distractions. That you are to be free from any interference. Actually say this out loud to both your body and your mind. Now start concentrating in your mind's eye.

3. Begin breathing with the usual technique - in through the mouth, out through the nose. With each breath that you breathe in, feel that you are bringing in love.

4. Visualize the love that you are bringing into your body and put it in your heart. Store the love in your body and do not allow it to escape. Allow it to float all through your body.

5. Visualize the love in your body running through your blood stream and coursing in your veins. Feel it moving within you, through ever fiber of your being. Feel the love completely saturate you from head to toe.

6. As you breath out, picture that you are releasing love into the world. You are breathing it in and releasing some out again, while storing love throughout your body. Visualize yourself being surrounded and bathed in love.

Practice this technique for about 20 minutes. You will feel refreshed when you are finished. Love is there for the taking, you just have to be receptive enough to receive it.

By receiving love, you will have a different outlook on life. You will appear more confident to other people and there will be an aura of love around you that will attract others. Meditating to receive love is one of the most relaxing and simplest of meditating techniques and it really does work.

The laws of attraction dictate that like attracts like. If you continue to bathe yourself in negative energy, you will receive negative responses in return. If, however, you choose to bathe yourself in love and positive energy, you will attract the same.

If you have someone who you love and want to draw them to you, picture them in your mind's eyes as you are meditating. Picture them loving you, caressing you, and being with you. Picture yourself loving them. You will be asking the universe to draw this person closer to you and the universe will respond, if you are receptive.

Love is something that no one should be without. There is too much of an abundance of love in the universe for anyone to be deprived of this bliss. You need only ask and you can mediate your way to love.

Chapter 11 - Meditate Yourself Free From Addiction

Are you addicted to drugs or alcohol? Do you know someone who is? Meditation can help anyone who is addicted to anything.

Approximately 30 percent of Americans claim to be addicted to something. Some are addicted to harmless things like video games or even the internet. Others are addicted to harmful narcotics. It is easy to see how being addicted to drugs can harm your life, but even "harmless" addictions are not so harmless when they start interfering with your life.

You can use meditation to break free from all types of addictions. The first step, however, is recognizing that you have a problem. Most addicts will deny that there is a problem with an addiction, despite being told by everyone that they know that they have a problem. They will deny that there is anything wrong with "them."

Eventually, all addicts reach a point in their lives where they hit rock bottom. When this happens, they have two ways to go - up or out. Hopefully, they choose up. It is at this point that an addict usually seeks help for his addiction.

No one can force an addict into recovery. All of the court orders in the world are not going to make an alcoholic become sober. The alcoholic has to truly want to be sober. Many alcoholics join Alcoholics Anonymous, an organization that has been very successful in helping people become sober.

Part of the mantra, if you will, of Alcoholics Anonymous is giving up the idea that you are in control of your life. Alcoholics Anonymous promotes giving your life to God and realizing that you can only control some aspects of your life. Meditation can work the same way. You may not be able to control everything in life, but meditation can allow you to control some aspects of your life.

When meditating to get rid of an addiction, it is important to realize that it will take some time. In addition to using meditation, you should also use any medication prescribed by your doctor. The meditation will help you in the long run, however, stay away from the addiction as well as get over the problem.

To meditate to get rid of an addiction, do the following:

1. Sit cross legged on the floor. Be conscious of your position. This is not a comfort meditation but one in which you will be conscious of your body. You will want to try the lotus position if at all possible. This may feel uncomfortable at first, but you will eventually get used to this position. The lotus position is a yoga position and is used as a way to contort your body. The purpose is to allow yourself to let go of the discomfort that your physical being is feeling.

2. Extend your hands upwards on your knees. This is a position that allows you to be open to the energy of the universe.

3. Think of a mantra. This should be one word. Choose a word that is positive and soothing at the same time.

4. Close your eyes and picture the object of your addiction. In your mind's eye, picture yourself tossing the addiction into a garbage can and getting rid of it, or tossing it off a bridge. Whatever works for you, but the objective is to get rid of the object.

5. Repeat the chant as you are doing this. Concentrate on the addiction being tossed away. Continue to repeat the chant with your eyes shut, palms up and in the same position. You should be ignoring any physical discomfort and not allowing your mind to wander. The chanting will become automatic.

Practice this for about 5 minutes at first. You can gradually work yourself up. Whenever the urge to drink or imbibe in your addiction hits you, resort to meditation. If you cannot meditate at that moment, repeat the chant, even if in you head. This will signal your mind to toss out the garbage.

Addictions are garbage. They are a negative impact in your life. Anything that keeps you from enjoying your life as well as others is detrimental to your psyche. You can eliminate an addiction simply by meditation.

Chapter 12 - Meditation To Cast Out Negativity

Is there someone in your life who is bringing you down? It can be a boss, co-worker or even an ex boyfriend or girlfriend. It can be a lost love who you still think about even though you know that they are gone from your life, or should be gone from your life.

Do you have negative thoughts that repeat themselves in your head? Negative thoughts are any thoughts that adversely affect your life. Perhaps you worry about illness, money or someone else. What do you do when you have these negative thoughts? Do you allow them to control your life?

Positive energy is all around you. Unfortunately, so is negative energy. But you needn't allow the negative energy that manifests in negative thoughts to interfere with your life. In order to be as productive as you can be, you have to remain positive.

You can choose to cast out negativity and be positive through meditation. Meditation to cast off unwanted thoughts of a person or event can work wonders. You can learn to reprocess your thought patterns so that you are not assaulted by negative images in your mind that give you a gloomy outlook on life and surround you with negative energy.

To cast off negativity, you can do the following:

1. Sit on the floor in the lotus position if possible with your palms up.

2. Close your eyes.

3. Think of the thing that is negative in your life that you wish to cast away. Repeat it out loud. If it is a person, for example, say their name out loud "John Smith."

4. Say "Out John Smith" or the name of the negative thing as your chant. You do not have to shout it, but it should be forceful.

5. Do not allow yourself to think about the negative person or thing. Concentrate instead on a picture in your mind's eye of you smiling and happy. Each time you think about John Smith, or the negativity, you will replace the negative image with the one of you smiling and happy.

6. In the meantime, you continue to say the name of the negative image until it becomes rote. This gives less meaning to the negativity. Your concentration should be all on yourself and your happy, smiling face.

The purpose of this meditation technique is to remove the importance of the negative influence that is in your life and make it insignificant. It is a mere chant that you are uttering, not anything real. What is real is in your mind and that is the picture of yourself laughing and smiling.

Chapter 13 - Meditation And Aromatherapy

In addition to meditation, aromatherapy is another Eastern healing art that has been used throughout the ages for a variety of different purposes. By incorporating aromatherapy into your meditation techniques, you can include the sense of smell and even taste into your meditation time.

In order to use aromatherapy in meditation, you will need to get an infuser. This is something that will burn essential oils. Essential oils are derived from natural substances such as bark, leaves, weeds, herbs, flowers and other natural objects. In order to realize the full healing potential of aromatherapy, you need to use 100 percent pure essential oils. These are available in a number of different places, including online outlets.

Essential oils work as you inhale them into your lungs. Their healing properties, when inhaled, are distributed throughout your body through your blood stream. There are over a hundred widely used essential oils. Each of them has different healing properties.

One of the most commonly used essential oils is lavender. Lavender is pretty much a heal-all remedy and is one of the safest essential oils to use. It has amazing healing powers.

Infusing an essential oil while meditating can compound the effect of meditation. It will also allow you to associate the scent with something pleasant. This association can be used when you are not able to meditate. For example, you can use a lavender scent at work so that you can remain positive throughout the day. You can even use synthetic lavender oils such as those that are found in perfumes and colognes to bring your scent with you through the day.

Using essential oils is yet another way that you can enjoy meditation to heal and improve your life.

Chapter 14 - Using Meditation To Improve Concentration

Attention deficit disorder is being diagnosed for many young people as well as adults. There are quite a few people both in the medical community and out that feel as though this condition is over diagnosed. Not everyone who has trouble concentrating had attention deficit disorder. But anyone who has trouble concentrating can use meditation as a way to improve their concentration.

Meditation can do wonders to improve your concentration. The average person has many different things on their mind at the same time. This consists of work, money, home, pleasure, family and even entertainment.

Naturally having all of these different thoughts running through your mind at the same time can cause you to be distracted. It can be difficult to concentrate on just one object at a time. Yet we all need to be able to focus if we want to be effective.

You can improve your concentration skills with meditation. In addition to improving your concentration, you can become more in tune with your senses as well as experience heightened spirituality.

To improve your concentration using meditation, do the following:

1. Sit in a comfortable position;
2. Focus on a particular object or photo
3. Use your energy to concentrate on the photo or object.

4. Put any other thoughts out of your head.
5. Each time you find yourself thinking of another thought, put it out of your head until your total concentration is on the object or photo.
6. Do this for 10 minutes

If you continue to meditate for ten minutes a day, you will gradually increase your concentration skills. You can train your brain to focus, you just have to have patience.

People who are unfamiliar with meditation mistakenly believe that it is all about making your mind go "blank." It is really about having more awareness - whether this is spiritual or just self awareness is up to you. If you choose to use a photo of a deity, you can use meditation as a form of prayer.

Chapter 15 - Practicing Meditation For A Healthy Life

Meditation is not something that you should just pick up and put down. It should be treated as more than just a passing fad - it should be a way of life for you. If you are going to practice meditation, you should make a commitment to practice for at least a month. This will give you plenty of time to discover whether or not this ancient practice is for you.

Notice the word "practice." No one gets to become an expert in meditation. Just as no one is perfect spiritually, no one can be perfect at meditation. There is always something else that you can learn about yourself when you practice meditation.

In addition to achieving a sense of calm and increasing your concentration and focus, you can do so much more with meditation. You will find that you have a better understanding of not only your personality, but the personality of others. You may discover that you have more compassion for other individual once you begin meditation.

In addition, your dreams will take on a new meaning. You will be better able to control your dream process and even enhance your dreams, such as lucid dreaming. Lucid dreaming is when you take control of your dreams in the dream state. You will find that you do this once in a while naturally, but when you start meditating, you will be able to have lucid dreams and an awareness even in your dream state. This allows you to transcend other planes.

Your senses will become more acute. You will feel everything differently once you are practicing meditation for a while. Everything that you smell, taste, see, feel and hear will have a new meaning for you. You will be more aware of your surroundings as well as other people.

In the world today, many people go around with their head in the clouds. They move through life in a fog, unaware of what other people are doing. They barely know themselves, let alone anyone else. We see people today who are disconnected from their families and even their children and spouse. Depression runs rampant amongst people who seem to have it all.

Meditation is hardly new. As stated in the beginning of this book, it is one of the oldest methods of healing in the world. It has been around for thousands of years and will most likely be around for thousands more.

Chapter 16 - Meditation Retreats and Lessons

Because meditation is becoming more accepted in the west as an alternate form of healing and method of well being, there are meditation retreats and conferences that you can join to learn how to practice meditation properly.

There are many different forms of meditation. Some meditate with the eyes closed, others with the eyes open. Some in a yoga position while others are in a position of comfort. Those who practice meditation believe that we can control our bodies with our mind.

Medical science holds many answers for us with regard to our health, but not all the answers. There are still many explanations that they do not have. There have been people who have received the benefits of what can only be termed a miracle when it comes to recovering from an illness.

One thing is certain that even the most hardened doctors will agree upon and that is that someone's emotional state has a lot of influence upon their physical health as well as their mental health. If you have a positive outlook in life, chances are that you will stay healthier. Studies prove that those who stay positive live longer, have lower blood pressure and even less disease. Stress really takes its toll on your body.

Instead of drugging yourself with pills to relieve stress, why not give meditation a shot? You really have nothing to lose but everything to gain from this experience. While this may not be for everyone, it is definitely worth a try. It certainly cannot hurt you.

Joining a meditation class does not have to be expensive. There are seminars and classes that are held all over the world. You can sign up for a weekend retreat to bring about inner peace and tranquility, or simply sign up for a class at your local gym. There are even classes held in some parks departments of towns.

Meditation does not have to be a spiritual journey, although it can be. And best of all, it can be a spiritual journey for any religion of your choice. Most religions practice some form of meditation. If you are praying, you are meditating.

Open your mind to a new possibility of healing and learning. Once you learn about this ancient art and the powers that are possessed in your mind, chances are that you will want to learn more about meditation. Fortunately, there are countless books and information that you can get on the internet that will teach you even more than you learned in this book.

This book on meditation is only the tip of the iceberg. It is enough to get you started in this practice, but cannot possibly tell you everything that you need to know about this practice. Such a book would fill up countless tomes.

One thing is certain and that is that you will not be any worse for the wear if you try meditation. But be prepared to give it a fair shot. Unlike pills, meditation is not the instant cure all. It does take time to get good at the techniques, but once you do, you will have greater clarity of thought, a better understanding of yourself, spiritual awareness and have the power to use your mind as you see fit.

Few people realize the potential they have in their mind. We have only a slight idea of what 75 percent of our brain does. Medical sciences has claimed that we only use a fraction of our minds. Suppose the cures that we seek are all within ourselves? It would make sense as nature seems to have provided everything we need to live. Why not provide our minds with healing power as well?

Taking a meditation class can be the best way to truly learn about the different techniques. Prior to signing up for a class, decide what you want to do. Do you want to:

- Gain a better insight of yourself?
- Learn to be calmer?
- Try to become a better person?
- Improve your concentration skills?
- Gain spiritual satisfaction?
- Be more in tune with your surroundings?
- Be more aware of your senses?
- Be more compassionate?
- Improve your communication skills?
- Overcome an addiction?
- Treat anxiety or depression?
- Alleviate stress?
- Transcend your dreams?

All of this and more can be taught to you when you take a meditation seminar. Take a look on the internet for meditation classes, books and other ways that you can learn how to meditate. Begin with this book and then get started on a journey into a whole new realm.

Your life will improve dramatically after you begin meditating. You will not only have a better understanding of yourself and your surroundings, but you will feel more in control of your own destiny.